The Alphabet Book

by Cheryl Ward

First edition, September 2023

ISBN 978-0-6452359-9-9

No Rest For The Wicked
norestforthewicked.net

NATIONAL
LIBRARY
OF AUSTRALIA

A catalogue record for this book is available from the National Library of Australia

The Alphabet Book

by Cheryl Ward

This book of alphabet illustrations came about when my daughter was six months old and I created these as a keepsake for her.

Enjoy discovering all the words and pictures scattered and highlighted throughout each illustration.

At the back of the book there are extra illustrations of some letters.

I hope you enjoy the book,
Cheers
Cheryl

enjoy!

abacus alien avocado alligator angle arch amphora almanac

alphabet aster anchovy arm abbey agate altar alfalfa

anchor apricot ant alarm ape artichoke acid

ambulance atom aspidistra arugula ash

apron artist adder attic anvil ace armadillo alley ant

anklet atlas axe amplifier acer anteater air agent amphibian

apple aurora angel artifact atrium almond ash

ankle arrow aeroplane acorn aqueduct

ball brother bicycle bath baby bell bean box barn

balloon butterfly beetle bracelet beach ...aker

bird blue band bones beaver bottle baggage

butter... barbecue bulb brown bank

black base block blind boot bib

beige blimp book blotch bull blue beast back br...

B

bush basement barracuda bus bat bomb bow blue

bacon balustrade building bin basket boat branch

cane corn cabbage car cork can coat caterpillar cricket cup cream cut circle card coconut chair coin check chameleon carpet candle cloud cat chart cloth capital clan crust cap cup croshatch chartreuse cow cyan cash curl castle cocoa cape cue camera clue cot cart carrot

diamond dinosaur duck dent doctor dirigible dots dance drill dingo desk dais drip dress desert drink dog dice dessert draughts dough daisy day dolphin dragonfly doll door dip dominoes duo

diagonal

E

emerald expert epilogue egg elves element elastic

ether eagle edit event ecru escalator election

eels effort eternity earring enamel email earth

endive eclair envelope evening escargot eggplant

fountain farm festival frog fork family **fish** finial flash frame fig

fleur-de-lys fashion flap fit fin fur filigree fiancee **flower**

flame foot finger fight flight forest fair fawn flash fen fashion fan flute flamingo file flannel **flower** fowl fact fence

flan father feast fairy flat finance fly figure football future flap flight fire frost frame face

fog funnel feet fete film fort frankfurter flea flavour fang garden ground goose globe garter grape ghost gong grasshopper gerbil goat gold guitar gecko goblet gopher giraffe gingham green grab garlic girl gander gel glove gargoyle glitter giant garbage glockenspiel ginger glasses gauntlet gnat gift gnu gang glass goldfish

gravel

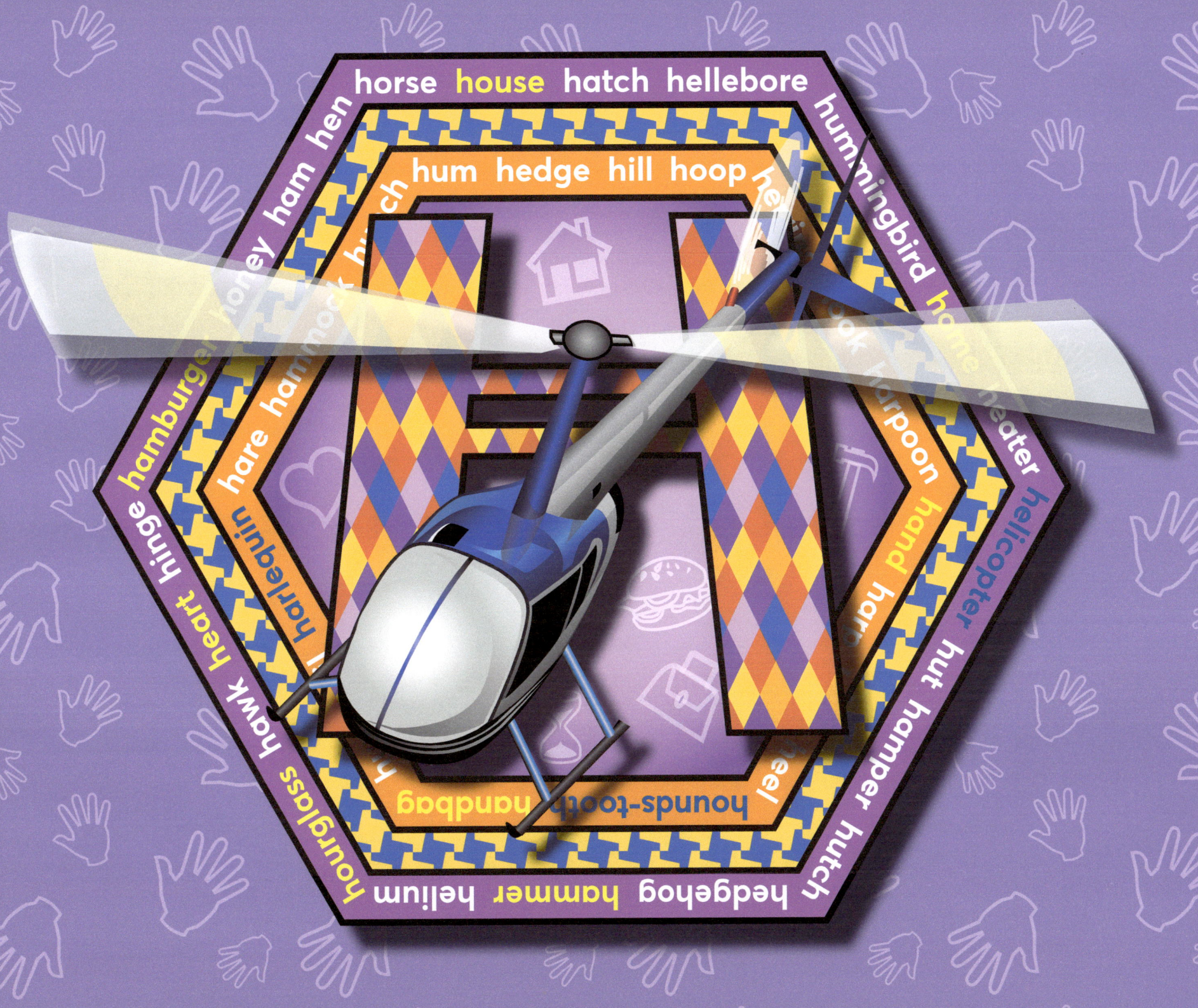

i

incense *isosceles* iron instep isolation ingot itch icon idle inner

iota *insects* isolation infant inch input instant income into

icicle

ice cream

imp island instrument invite

innings ibex imprint infinity idol isobar

inferno information inflammation Isotope iguana isle indent iceberg

inchworm it ink

impatiens inn incident index icy inlet international inlay

ice identity ice inhabitants ibis italic item insignia iguana ivory ivy

ice cube

jack-in-the-box jam joker jungle jade jumble jiggle

joke jackpot joust jump jet jasper jiffy jingle

jackal jeweler jacket juice jinx judge jail jewel

jellybean jut jury jest

jumper jug jive jacks

jewelery jonquil jerboa

junket jay jester jam jaguar judgement jacaranda

jeep junk jazz jigsaw javelin jasmine jellyfish

justification joint jeans jaunt jelly jaundice

justice juggernaut

kangaroo kite keg kitchen kiss kiosk koala knight kookaburra kindling kit knee kaleidoscope kind kettle kiln knock key knife kayak kilt khaki knot knuckle knitting kiwi

locomotive lily lap lamp lobster lasagne leather lute leaf leak
lucite legume lozenge louse loophole lash lizard lucerne
lever lighthouse listen look laugh light lettuce litter lung lioness left lightyear lightyear ledge
lucite legume lozenge louse loophole lash lizard lucerne
labyrinth lace lip lick lattice label llama lamprey legend lump lodge low
loch lagoon lemur langoustine lard law lemming lionfish
lunge lift lunge lunge lemon ladder leek loin lasso lounge lock lion lemonade law lard langoustine lemur lagoon loch
lemon

magnet moon microscope moose master machine map monster mole money moat melon metal manatee miss meteor meet mug minute mouth method mitt mask metronome mosaic magenta missile music mushroom match molecule marmot moth mouse medal mauve magpie mess mast myth melt mead mermaid mountain marble microphone mathematics monkey

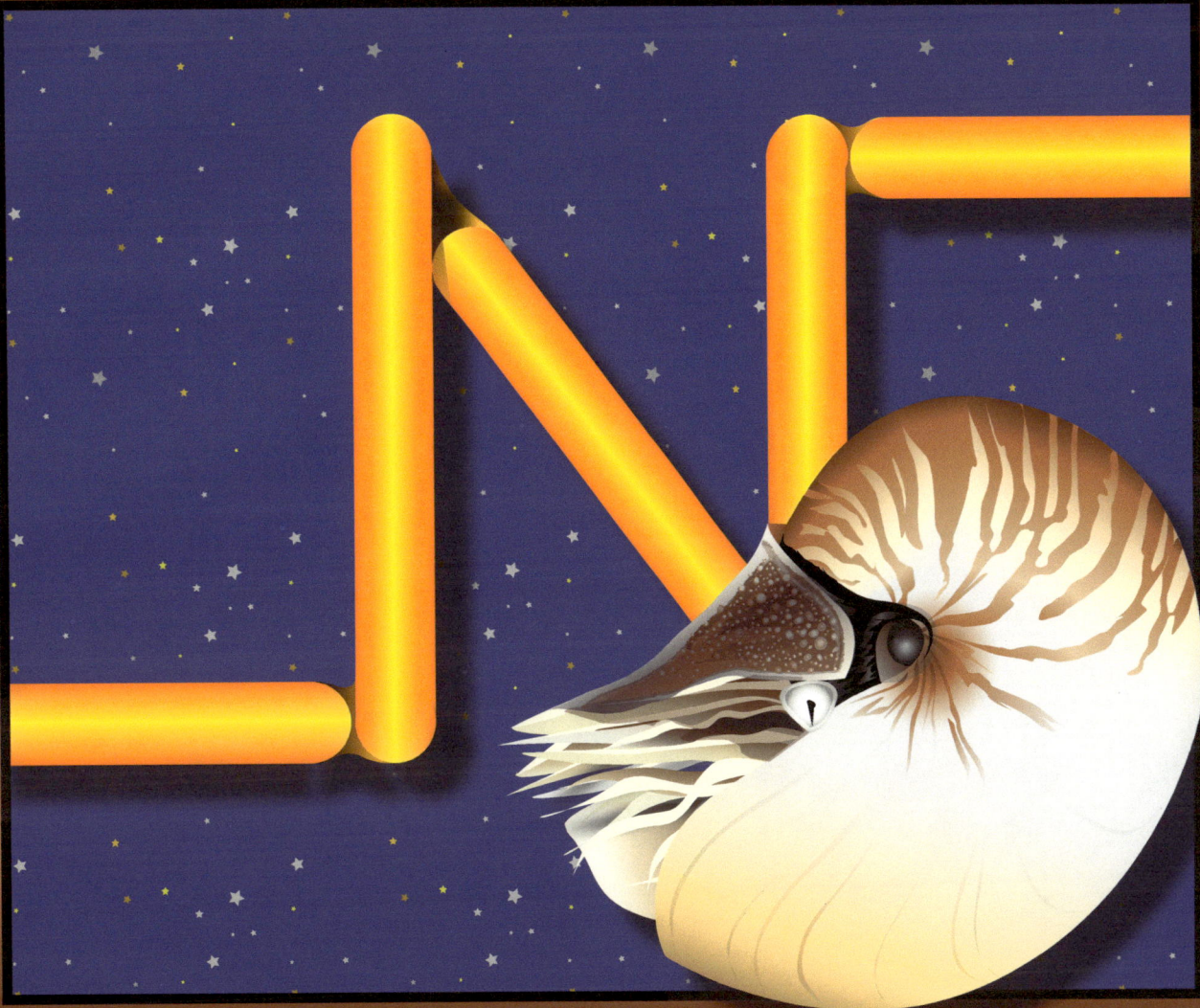

noodle newt newspaper notice north numbat nimbus noise
nephew noon niece nautilus nougat nut nerve nurse
noodle nodule nuance nurture novel nuance
nought night ninja nodule
necktie nature nectar nest night
nail net nominate nurture novel
necktie nature
number neon nose nought network now
none note ninth name noose night near nice
nightie nitrogen never noun nap nightingale narwhal
neck napkin nugget navel needle necklace nose nutmeg navy

O

olive owl octagon okra oasis oboe onyx odour overcoat oxygen omega otter okapi oyster orca oregano oxen octopus ocean oatmeal operation ostrich octet organ orange ocelot onion oak orangutan orchid oil orchestra oryx omelet oblong oat oracle ottoman oar omega ormolu osprey oval organza overt oar operation omega oar

owl

parcel patchwork

pack pale

pine puggle

platypus plum

pattern pond

peach possum

pumpkin pest

parquet paisley

pentagon parrot

play pug

pebbles purple

pin penguin poster

paint pitch pot pooch

pen pit pirate panda pencil pink

pear

quote quail quotidian quota quill quantity queue

quest quarter quiff quiet quoit quadrant quilt

quote quail quotidian quota quill quantity queue

quip quaver quit quince question quite queen

quadrille quart quasi quid quoth quack quaff que

To be or not to be

R

rower **rain** racquet refrigerator rind **red** right relocate relay ruler

role rag reindeer rhododendron rip reflector robot ray rust

robot **rose** radar record ring radish ramp rot

ram **ruby** risk rug rattle railway rocket

rainbow race raccoon ribbon rickshaw rip

asp rubble radicchio ridge rickshaw

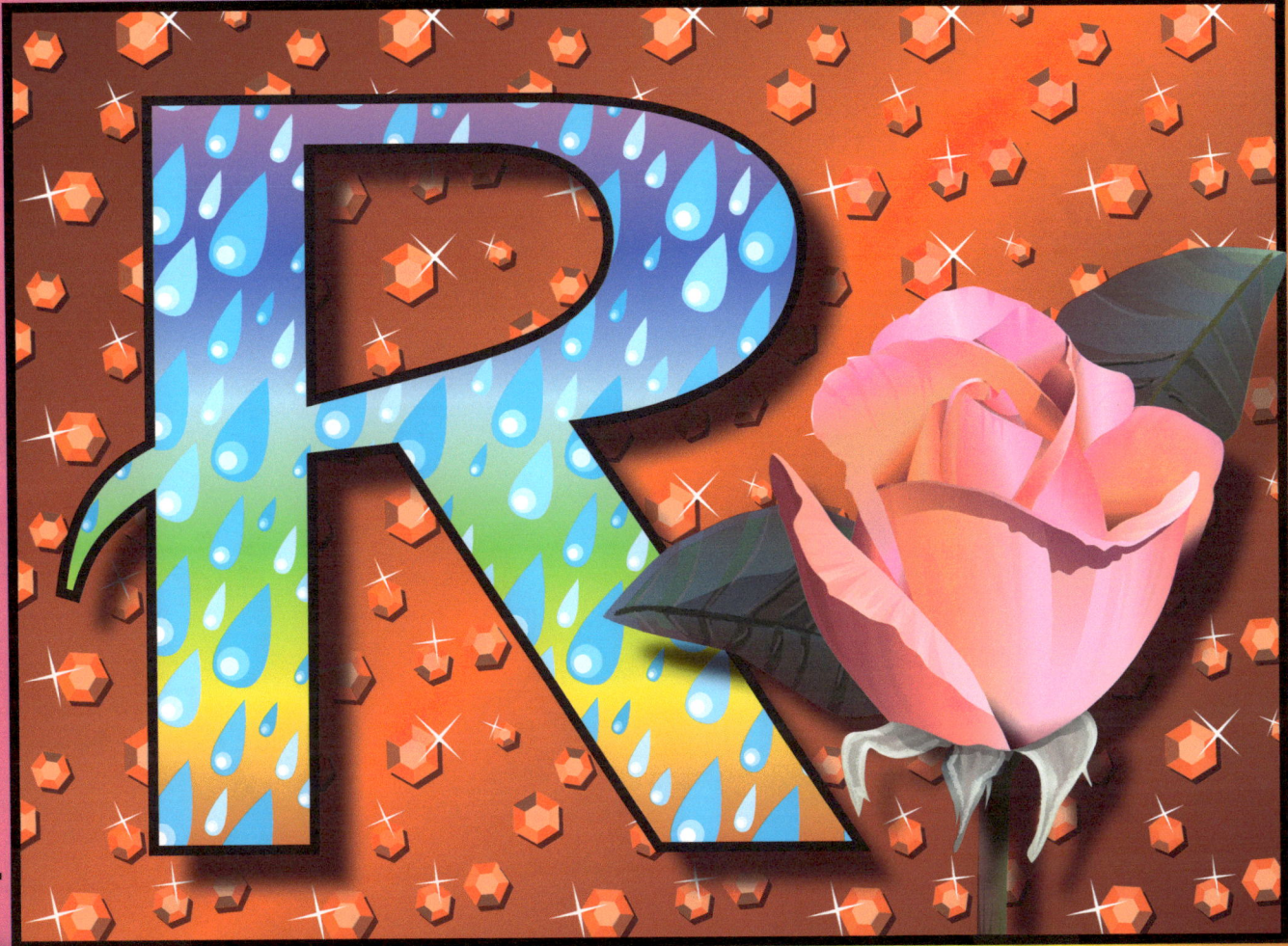

rat recorder rope rhubarb row right-angle rebound rhinoceros

raspberry root **rectangle** rabbit rooster rapids rodeo reflector

rock

tickle top

turtle

top

triangle taste

tablet treat

tartan

twig

taffeta

toucan trumpet tangerine tangle trap tightrope tea table target trestle

teal tuba two

unicorn **umbrella** umpire UFO uniform uphill use

university uncle underpass useless

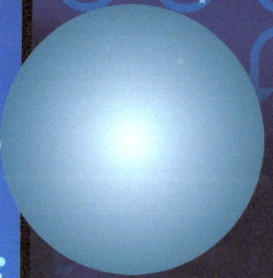

ultramarine urn u-turn ukulele

ugly useful unusual

universe uranium upper ugh

undulation

undo

universe

uranium

undulation

undo

uranus

vine votive valise vinegar vegemite valve valid vessel verve vapid
vestige village visage violin vault view voter viola vignette

velvet vegetable vermilion vase venison valet vehicle vintage vet violet vindication vim

V

vacuum vent voltage valour vicar victim vestibule valley volatile veal vitamin van

vest valour vicar

vulture vegan viking vane vicarage video vacancy variation victual

vice vampire voice vein volcano viaduct victory villa vehicle

xyolgraph xeric x xenon xmas x-chromosome xylophone x x-ray xenophobe xanthippe xanthous xenothith xerox x xxl xl xs x

Xerochrysum
Bracteatum

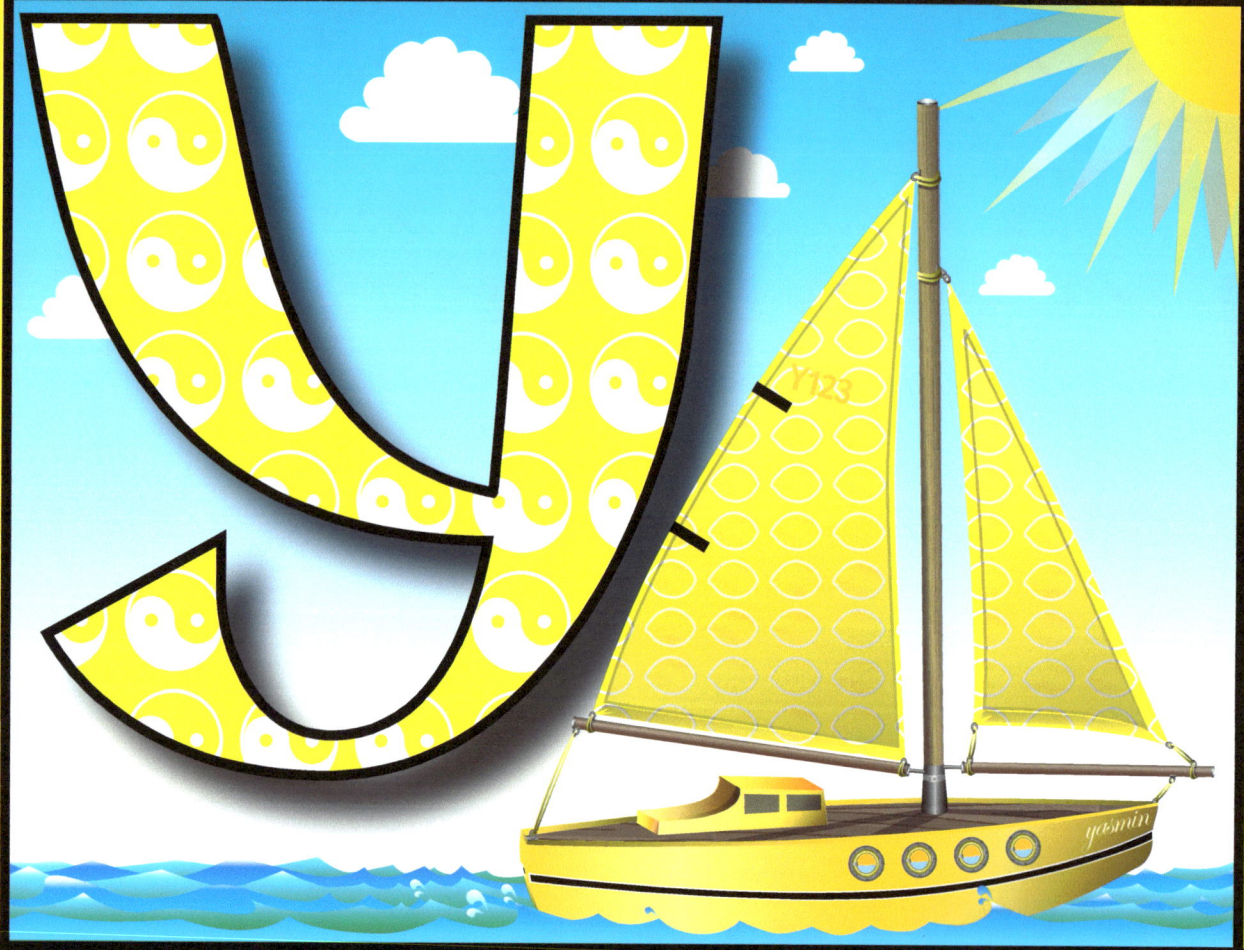

yeoman you yet youthful yoghurt yonder yurt yam yes

yellow yak yacht yell yeti year yodel

yesterday yell yawn yo-yo ying-yang

zulu **zebra** zing zany **zinc** zipper zeppelin zoom zzz

zinnia **zigzag** zodiac zone zabaglione zoo zzz

zither zealous zen zoetrope zing

ziggurat zip-line zany zephyr zinc zipper zepplin zoom zip

Z

EXTRA

LETTERS

A

eyelet engine earnings easter egg essay earphones exit earplug escape elevator eleven escalator effect electricity ear echidna easel ellipse emu elf ewer eagle emblem envelope early entry earwig endocrine ester earl eucalypt enjoyment enchilada eggcup elk eclipse eclair emerald eon east ego eggshell eatery equipment emotion

Eucalyptus

H

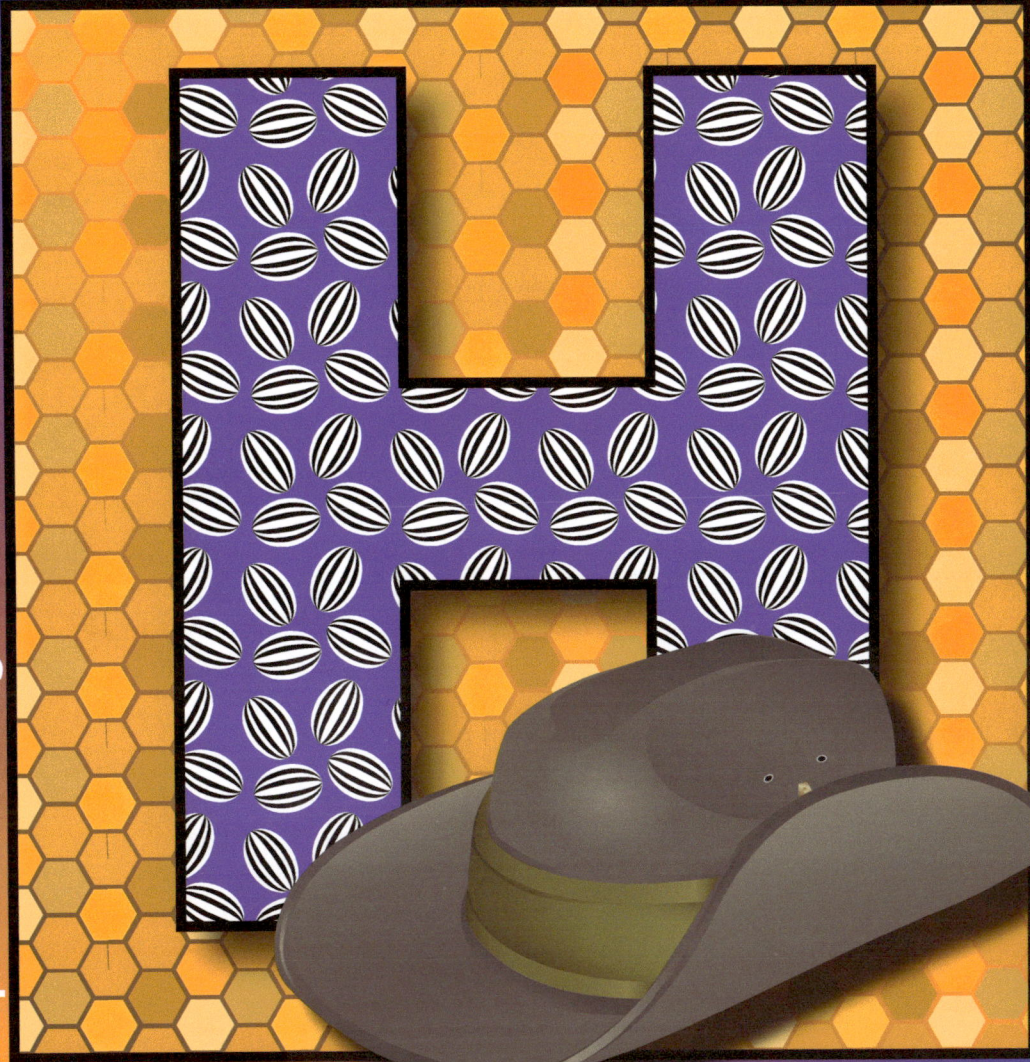

heliotrope human heel hunter highlight hut haste

handicraft hearing hour hover haggis heath

honeycomb hero history halibut hat hinge humbug health

hexagonal hug hips handle

halo hospital horse hound hop hedge heron

head hail helm heater harness hiccup hollow hag

hem hippopotamus humble herringbone helix

hoist hotel hoop herd hanger hopscotch

library lunch lemon lavender ledge lollipop lead lip laundry love locket look lift land loop lacquer lozenge logo lashes laser lance lilac

lapse luge leadlight loch lawn lizard lemur lane lesson loans lyrics lore lilo lounge lunar like led lung leg lottery lipstick lake laugh lead lips lawn list

N

numb neat nourishing next number newborn nettle nip nearby nostril numerical nemesis nervous necessity neutral notable nudibranch nachos nudge nouse nappy necessary nimble nowhere new notification news nocturnal nine nasty nectarine neap nigella net neckerchief nineteen

1 2 3 4 5 6 7 8 9 10

salmon satin starfish scarf spaghetti shade scratch

stamp spin saddle sun shell sale siphon salt

silk spoon sea slate

satellite skid sword

salad swift smell stitch squid sugar sap

swamp seat sunrise silver sandwich snail sleet

stirrup stake skates scales street sand

star surf spell

seaweed spice ship spatchcock shuttle

sugar sarsaparilla stick saffron stamp square

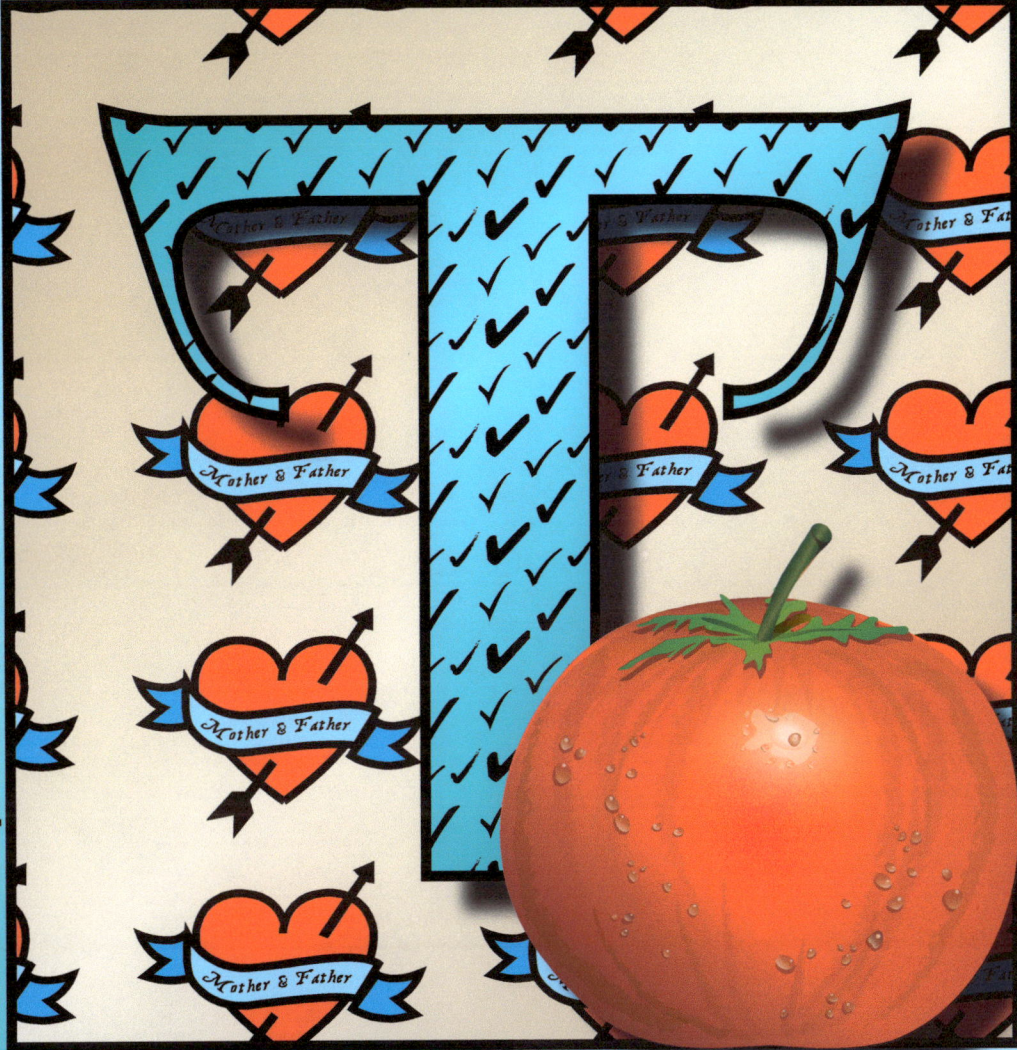

toadstool tightrope tights tomato tiger twilight tick
treat teacher tympanum tot toast town twig
tinsel tickets tower thatch tantrum transept tick tint
treaty trumpet transit trapeze toll tuna typewriter toga
tattoo twin twill tickle toaster
tool tone toe top-hat tan tomboy tonsil trait
twister turquoise tambourine train troll trefoil tissue
tour tin time taupe thatch tantrum transept tick tint
tram tropical

www.ingramcontent.com/pod-product-compliance
Lightning Source LLC
Chambersburg PA
CBHW040404100426

42811CB00017B/1829